Look

A Reading Anthology for Young Learners

LUCY CRICHTON

NATIONAL
GEOGRAPHIC
LEARNING

Australia • Brazil • Mexico • Singapore • United Kingdom • United States

1

Contents

1   Click! Click! 3

2   The Granny Cloud 9

3   We're All Superheroes! 15

4   Where's Rosie? 21

5   The Farmer and the Rock 27

6   A Sandy Surprise 35

    Activities 42

4

5

8

The Granny Cloud

This is a school in India. The children want to learn English.

"I have an idea!" says the teacher.

"Let's talk to a granny who speaks English! We can use a computer."

"This is called the Granny Cloud," says the teacher.

"We can talk to a granny in a different country and learn English."

"Hello!" says the lady. "How are you?"

"We're fine, thank you. We want to learn English!"

"Wonderful! I can help you."

They speak English with her every week. She's very happy to help them.

Soon, a lot of children in different schools talk to the Granny Cloud.

We're All Superheroes!

I'm a superhero!

This is what I have:

A special red cape.

It helps me a lot!

I have strong arms.

This is so much fun!

I have strong legs

To run, run, run!

I have long hair

And blue, blue eyes.

I'm a super superhero.

Watch me fly!

This is my super body,

This is my star.

I can help you

Wherever you are!

This is my super smile,

These are my ears.

If you are sad,

I am near!

I'm ready for the world!

Look at me and see.

I'm a super superhero,

That's what I want to be!

Where's Rosie?

Ben lives on a farm. He has a pet sheep.
Her name's Rosie.

Ben loves Rosie. She follows him everywhere!

One day, Ben can't find Rosie. Where is she?

Maybe she's under the tree.

There's a goat under the tree, but I can't find Rosie!

Maybe she's in the flowers.

There's a cat in the flowers, but I can't find Rosie!

Maybe she's in the pond. Oh no! She can't swim!

There are ducks in the pond, but I can't find Rosie!

Oh no! Where's Rosie?

There she is!

Baa!

Oh Rosie! I'm so happy to see you!

The Farmer and the Rock

There's a big rock in the road.

One day, a man walks down the road.
He can't go past the rock.

The next day, two women walk down the road.
They can't go past the rock.

Now everyone can get by.

33

Now everyone thanks the farmer for being kind.

A Sandy Surprise

Edu, Sam, Lara, and Silvia are friends. It's summer vacation. They're at the beach.

36

38

41

STORY 1 Click! Click!

Match and write.

1.

What's this?

It's a _____.

2.

What's this?

It's a _pencil_____.

3.

What's this?

It's a _____.

4.

What's this?

It's a _____.

STORY 2 The Granny Cloud

Look and write.

It's a book.   How many dogs?
It's orange and blue.   ~~How are you?~~

1.
Hello! _How are you?_

I'm fine, thanks.

2.
What's this?

_____

3.
_____

Three.

4.
What color is your uniform?

_____

43

We're All Superheroes!

Look and write.

super body ~~strong arms~~ blue eyes strong legs

2. These are my
_____.

3. These are my
_____.

1. These are my
strong arms____.

4. This is my
_____.

Where's Rosie?

Look, read, and circle.

1.

   There's / (There are)
   three white ducks in
   the pond.

2.

   There's / There are
   two goats under a tree.

3.

   There's / There are
   a cat in the flowers.

4.

   There's / There are
   a donkey in a field.

The Farmer and the Rock

Look and answer *Yes, it is* or *Yes, they are.*

1. Are these your pants?

Yes, they are.

2. Is this your dress?

_____

3. Is this your skirt?

_____

4. Are these your jewels?

_____

A Sandy Surprise

Look and answer.

~~Yes, there is.~~   No, there isn't.
No, there aren't.   Yes, there are.

1. Is there a sand jellyfish on the beach?

   Yes, there is.

2. Are there boats in the ocean?

   _____

3. Are there four sun hats?

   _____

4. Is there a sandcastle on the beach?

   _____

NATIONAL GEOGRAPHIC
L E A R N I N G

National Geographic Learning,
a Cengage Company

***Look 1: A Reading Anthology for
Young Learners***
Lucy Crichton

Publisher: Sherrise Roehr

Executive Editor: Eugenia Corbo

Publishing Consultant: Karen Spiller

Senior Development Editor: Mary Whittemore

Associate Development Editor: Jen Williams-Rapa

Director of Global Marketing: Ian Martin

Heads of Strategic Marketing:

    Charlotte Ellis (Europe, Middle East
    and Africa)

    Kiel Hamm (Asia)

    Irina Pereyra (Latin America)

Product Marketing Manager: David Spain

Senior Director of Production: Michael Burggren

Senior Content Project Manager: Nick Ventullo

Media Researchers: Leila Hishmeh, Jeff Millies

Art Director: Brenda Carmichael

Manufacturing Planner: Mary Beth Hennebury

Composition: SPi Global

For permission to use material from this text or product,
submit all requests online at **cengage.com/permissions**
Further permissions questions can be emailed to
permissionrequest@cengage.com

ISBN: 978-0-357-02751-6

National Geographic Learning
20 Channel Center Street
Boston, MA 02210
USA

Locate your local office at **international.cengage.com/region**

Visit National Geographic Learning online at **ELTNGL.com**
Visit our corporate website at **www.cengage.com**

Credits

Cover: © Frans Lanting/Mint Images/Getty Images.

Photos: 3 © bofotolux/Shutterstock.com; **4** © Pashin Georgiy/Shutterstock.com; **5** © Adrian Candela/Shutterstock.com;
6 © freedomnaruk/Shutterstock.com; **7** © Syda Productions/Shutterstock.com ; **9** David South/Alamy Stock Photos;
10 © Barcroft/Getty Images; **11** © Barcroft/Getty Images; **12** © Barcroft/Getty Images; **13** © Barcroft/Getty Images;
14 (t, b) © Barcroft/Getty Images; **15** © Rawpixel.com/Shutterstock.com; **16** © Rawpixel.com/Shutterstock.com; **17** © Yuganov
Konstantin/Shutterstock.com; **18** © Yuganov Konstantin/Shutterstock.com; **19** © Rawpixel.com/Shutterstock.com;
19 (background) © Elenamiv/Shutterstock.com; **20** © Srijaroen/Shutterstock.com; **42** (tl) © Thithawat.S/Shutterstock.com;
42 (tr, mbl) © Kidsada Manchinda/Shutterstock.com; **42** (mtl) © binbeter/Shutterstock.com; **42** (mtr) © studiovin/
Shutterstock.com; **42** (mbl) © Elnur/Shutterstock.com; **42** (bl) © pelfophoto/Shutterstock.com; **42** (br) © Kletr/Shutterstock.com;
45 (t) © ThePoii/Shutterstock.com; **45** (mt) © Lukasz Pawel Szczepanski/Shutterstock.com; **45** (mb) © Andrew Hagen/
Shutterstock.com; **45** (b) © Robcartorres/Shutterstock.com.

Illustrations: 3–8 Holly Hatam/CATugeau; **21–26** Morgan Huff/Bright Agency; **27-34, 46** Turine Tran/Illustration Web; **35–41,
47** Katy Betz/CATugeau; **43** Kim Soderberg/Illustration Online; **44** Martina Crepulija/Illustration Online.

Print Number: 10   Print Year: 2024
Printed in Mexico